VANCOUVER FOR BEGINNERS

VANCOUVER FOR BEGINNERS

ALEX LESLIE

BOOK*HUG PRESS 2019

The production of this book was made possible through the generous assistance of the Canada Council for the Arts and the Ontario Arts Council. Book*hug Press also acknowledges the support of the Government of Canada through the Canada Book Fund and the Government of Ontario through the Ontario Book Publishing Tax Credit and the Ontario Book Fund.

 Canada Council **Conseil des Arts**
for the Arts **du Canada**

Funded by the   Financé par le
Government   gouvernement
of Canada   du Canada | Canada

 **ONTARIO ARTS COUNCIL**
CONSEIL DES ARTS DE L'ONTARIO
an Ontario government agency
un organisme du gouvernement de l'Ontario

Book*hug Press acknowledges the land on which it operates. For thousands of years it has been the traditional land of the Huron-Wendat, the Seneca, and most recently, the Mississaugas of the Credit River. Today, this meeting place is still the home to many Indigenous people from across Turtle Island, and we are grateful to have the opportunity to work on this land.

Library and Archives Canada Cataloguing in Publication

Title: Vancouver for beginners / Alex Leslie.
Names: Leslie, Alex (Mystery story writer), author.
Identifiers: Canadiana (print) 20190158069 | Canadiana (ebook) 20190158093
    ISBN 9781771665346 (softcover) | ISBN 9781771665353 (HTML)
    ISBN 9781771665360 (PDF) | ISBN 9781771665377 (Kindle)
Classification: LCC PS8623.E845 V36 2019 | DDC C811/.6—dc23

PRINTED IN CANADA

"Perhaps, Kublai thought, the empire is nothing but a zodiac of the mind's phantasms."
—Italo Calvino, *Invisible Cities*

"The sky above the port was the colour of television, tuned to a dead station."
—William Gibson

CONTENTS

1.
ENTER BY THE RIVERS OR INLET

RAINFOREST PARADISE

Now that there is no weather there are only trends. Roots knit an urban basket. This was all forest way back when. Old-growth towers, glass swan spines. Public parks in buckets line the curbs for pickup. Recycling mecca, whose residents eat compost with full cream and push the poor from rooftop gardens into moss that flows from the lips of dumpsters, ocean dreaming in the background, mountains offering shadows to lean into, a sheltered city pillaged for bed frames. The forest's understory inhales, creeks shout from the manholes, on public transit a wavesounds meditation CD has been playing on loop for 180 years. Born into this misty static, residents swing axes at each other's ankles and fall like saplings into Taiwan-bound barges and post-industrial wet dreams, into hammocks knit from track-marked cedar branches. Hydroponic lovers nest in shore phone booths, a bulldozer uncurls its sleepy head and splits the street open with an egg tooth. At night raccoons patrol the valleys and alleyways with the cops, obligatory ravens wing-to-wing down the wires, and a man pushes a shopping cart full of huckleberry plants, salal, and prehistoric ferns toward the bottle depot. On his off-nights he is a flamethrower.

MOUTH OF THE FRASER RIVER

Because our thirst is never satisfied, a pipeline runs through us. The ex-river widened for your use. Riverbed, sidewalk, gutterpath. Land deveined of creeks with one swift tug. Old flow, a long tear down the surface visible only from the bridge. The ex-river runs a path dug by moonlight. Marine Drive, spook of delta. At the mouth of the ex-river, where it empties and spreads, a gate installed by the Department of Fisheries and Oceans. The ex-river slips through iron grates, slithers among pipes under bedrooms and kitchens. Do not try to take care of the river. Take care of what is around the river and the river will take of itself, instructs the pamphlet released by the city. A manhole gargles, coughs uphill from the water table. A dog lumbers the blackberry path, pants sugary heat. A city engineer crawls, green aluminum fins pinned to his ankles, rubs his belly on the pavement, a compass in his teeth. A salmon with small dark stones for eyes hurtles forward to her home above the reservoir, to the second Vancouver trapped in the clouds. Inside the ex-river, glass fishing floats whirl, each one an eye closing. Autumn is eternal. The ex-river skin slick with crimson handprints. Vancouver opens its mouth and words come out. When you drink from the river, you forget.

FOREST FIRE SEASON

Today the city lies on its back, its stomach bled out.

Buildings hang upside down. Windows plate the harbour.

Trees send roots upward thirsting for chemical reservoir.

Bridges dangle from the inlet's dark wrists.

This morning the city tilts its head in a heat dream blown in
from the other side.

Crazy-eye sun bores a hole through orange fog.

The city lies on its back on a new bed this morning.

Dreams itself in the bay lit up with pickled afterbirth.

Every sunset colour in the new alien dust-clouds descends.

The city lies on its back on the old, thinking cool of the channel.

What's underneath is forced upward and flips.

Houses inverted under the nuclear lid.

A lung suspended in a yellow cloud chamber.

Yellow so listless you could stare into it forever and not go blind.

BARTER

In the news today: Vancouver is tearing down the art gallery that used to be the land registry. The barge that unloads the hybrid cars leaves full of cedar, fat roots like fingers in the oil slick due north. The trawler's hold unloads flash-frozen salmon, departs full of clouds and tickets. The beach sealed with a wall had its lip peeled back, and a new shore named Water Street installed. The courthouse converted into a killing bazaar where bear furs are exchanged for oil paintings of possessed trees rebelling within a glass house, seizuring apparitions the shades of a coastal storm. This fentanyl can be traded for eclipse. People do not come here to buy and sell but for miraculous business. Once a week crowds gather on the street and make their offerings: a van full of mixed wire; a Bible with half the words blacked out, *extra charge for the editing*. Forest of pipes traded for a river. First city bartered for a struck match. An inlet for a swimming pool named prosperity, dosing fentanyl into the veins of a chemical dawn. And somewhere back there, the past was traded for a different past. Vancouver releases its plan for the new art gallery: it will be built near the old viaduct, a fresh bamboo temple where wood was traded for blood.

INLET ECHOCARDIOGRAM

Inside acoustics. Ocean on shuffle
drained nightly, a new tide
spelled on the city's burnt edge.
Horizon control
soundbox, throats buffer
names, crossfade to
the flesh. Score
wiped again and swimming out
into blind tidal wiring. Wrists
bound and kelp.
In the dark, echoes sensormurmur
homing signals from glowing
chests of commuter
whales
bellies of Toyotas
and
greenwood.

Repeat from the beginning.

English Bay refills with static, scrubs
the skin of a freighter pregnant
with enough oil to render
this scrapyard edge of the
Pacific uninhabitable
for the next two hundred years.
Downbeat.
The microphones

were placed
in Vancouver's
inhabitants' chests
at birth.

The inlet
works a
cabled arm
into the city's
centre,
tectonic spin
on the pelvic floor
sinks chambers
into the temporary
foundation. The shallows
burrow under the bridges
that staple
the city's
stomach.

Inhabitants
go under again
for a season
bass line shoehorned
from a foghorn's
blue mind,

morning massaged from stone.
Old fishermen
line the shore with buckets,
clearing computer chips and omens.

Looptrack
of tide
on synth
eardrum
fibrillates.
Ear
pressed
to the
blasting
ground.

Ocean is
analog.

LOVERS

Go down to the old port on Valentine's Day to see streets burned in the Great Fire of 1886 resurrected by the city for tourists. Singed cedar arcs, the brothel a stage on peg legs, an actress screaming in the background, hurling her body every twelve minutes into the waves that brief the saltlick shore beyond the overpass. She arrives at daybreak, slams her cityblock shoulders into the surf. People on the opposing shore raise their fists in welcome. She has worked this shore for centuries, knows where to unbutton the waves.

A cruise ship drifts by and releases nets, snags her hair and discarded fingernails, dumps out a hook and a trunk of bent keys. She returns to shore, phosphorescence turning turning turning in her womb, opens her mouth, eyes shedding dark fish, generations of salmon flop into the buckets crowded in foam. The tourists arrive in families, spread beach towels on sunlit slagheaps, stretch limbs, watch her do laps, turn their faces from the streets scrubbed of graffiti and the past.

For this one day, from the gutters scorched with hotel bleach and blood-pinked brine, from the black roofs and shuddering wooden boardwalks polished by the commerce of men's boots. They watch her swim, body arched graceful as a whale toward the open ocean toward the silent tanker barricade toward the series of bridges that link us, a wavering spinal chain in silhouette one two three.

POSTCARD HOME FROM ENGLISH BAY

Nostalgia is a territory. Chain-smoking seagulls do yoga on the horizon at dawn. English Bay organized into lanes with flaming buoys for swimmers to do their drive-by banking. The bridge shut down for candidates who launch down the inlet on robotic wings, competing for votes. People tread water below to witness, swallow the new Pacific vaccine. The famous building with the tree growing out of its roof drinks rainwater, spits mercury into the teacups of developers. Acid rain rainbows the parade tie-dye, the marchers photograph their chemical shadows and post in Renaissance filter, reflections in oil paints. Pride bellyflops into a harbour of profit. The portrait artist hired by the mayor works until sunset, then lies down in the surf and dissolves, skin floating off clear as a jellyfish, black formal tails trailing ink. It is so beautiful here. This child will draw your caricature for free by throwing a glass of coins in your face and raising his fingers to catch the bent light that arcs off your cheekbones. Blink and you'll miss the moon inspecting its own bruises, reading Captain Vancouver's letters home by the lights of a thousand rigs, miniatures available in bottles for collectors and investors. Visit soon.

MARPOLE BUS LOOP

Whales sleep in the bus loop at night. Orcas loll on the asphalt, black skins thump oil-drum hymnals, they swim up from their old sleeping under the hollows to rest where men built the parking lot to hold the buses for this coast city. Paved over the cabled grass, shell, ground-up vertebrae, old berths in saltwater belly, the city's fleets of buses sleep here under the Laing Bridge's flare of light, a pod of eighteenth-century engines sunk into muck, rusted out with river pulp. Pacific commuter blood vessels homing to mammalian bed, hubcap eyes blinking between the branches of the Fraser, mouths push out smoke, dawn shorefogs stuffed with gull wings, motorcycle motors and rage, windshields muzzled with fog. The buses have been coming here for centuries, sleeping off the work of a river unzipping its skin, sloughing birdland, shedding flatgrass, dropping their skins on the shale city edges, fat flensed off curbs. The buses moan, lean into one another for warmth, rub barnacles on steel, the old wartime trolly cables telegraph sea songs. Guttered melody in the pipes. Another dead one found in English Bay this morning, oil spill off sunset, whale with a chemical half-life. The inlet rinses its morning mouth with bunker fuel and spits out streets. A bus breached off Lion's Gate. A thousand phones captured its slow soar. The tankers are calving, birth matter flowers ochre in the bay. A net hangs over the foot of Burrard for any stray life. No one wants to go into the ocean this summer. Out there, the buses drink black milk in the deep. The nightshift drivers park the whales belly-to-belly in the lot under the bridge. Whales roll in the shallows, flip steel dorsals, bask in the spume from the wheels on Marine Drive, chew up tickets and ferns and midden, their eyes fade to rings of knowing delta grey. At sunrise, the whales head off on their daily transit routes, haul their bodies up Granville past the library, vegetable stands, apartment blocks. The power grid is the new coastline. Their wide-open headlights half-lit in the ocean-bottom streets, halogen eyes stare at tumbled logs roiling at the base of the city's industrial throat. The buses head off for the day and gather up people in flocks, all the way up the hill. All the whales are singing and rolling down there at the bottom of Marpole in the unmarked graveyard where they park the buses.

SWIMMING ADVISORY

Riptide. Seachange at dawn. Take

precautions. Jumpers rarely retrieved.

Fast lane; medium lane; tanker lane.

Radioactive ghosts blow in from Japan.

Lifeguard on duty in his

red sleep on the rocks;

do not disturb marine life. Fire ban. No harvesting

by order of medical officer.

Bunker fuel. Algae bloom solar

in the deep. Seals on leashes, dogs

rippled with dental kelp. Enter these waters

and emerge changed. November beaches

barren as the moon, white laneways

to the bridges. Salt farm. No

diving. Buoys ride the hidden shelf. Washed in:

a cup, a foot, glass fishing floats

with late-stage glaucoma, dead stare. If in a state of

distress, float. Open your arms, ride on the

water's wide black back, catamaran human. Stay out

of tanker traffic, radio for help, commit to memory

the channel. Data crawl on the ocean floor

brings up nothing. In the corner

of your eye, orange construction cranes

pray to the mountains for new life. Iris scan.

Naked lunch at the point. A man named Truth Lizard

has lived on this beach since the '70s.

Never swim here. At night extreme swimmers bump

up against the boats. Every day it is

forty-five minutes later. Swimmers orbit

the moon as a slow street

circles the settlement.

August—

driftwood thighs,

driftwood shoulders,

driftwood asses

arranged by the fulcrum

hand of tide. Dune lips. Pursed around

light. Bay hot with bodies. Front-crawl to the shallows.

Barnacles maul your burns.

Limited visibility. Between the crying

of waves, the city never happened.

Beyond the point, blindness.

Past fog. Out there a woman is floating

in the depths, a coin

over each eye.

USER'S MANUAL

This is not

        a guidebook
        a real estate listing
        a warning
        an omen
        a memoir
        an environmental survey
        a map
        a goodbye letter
        a love letter
        to my hometown

This is not

        a letter to the estate
        a map of omens
        a loveguide to warnings
        a memoir of goodbyes
        an environment

This is not

        a warning guide
        a goodbye to environment
        a love of omens
        a hometown book
        an estate's memoir
        a letter

2.
DEVELOPMENT APPLICATION

DEVELOPMENT APPLICATION #1

TO BE POSTED IN A PROMINENT PLACE ON A
WELL-TRAFFICKED URBAN BEACH FOR A MINIMUM
OF SIXTY DAYS PRIOR TO DRILLING

The Pacific was born today and let me tell you how. The city planted in the hole in the floor of the ocean blocks the freefall that comes from under. The first city made of bedrock before the ocean boiled, softening the stone. The second city, the government-issued replacement, is steel reinforced with an alloy of promises. The first city was featured in a number of stories understood as metaphors in the way an alloy, as a combination of forces, is a metaphor for strength, and the ocean is a metaphor for itself, pronounced ---------. The second city will be installed via a nighttime excursion through black-scarved water, the cloudy lit heads of judges riding inlet currents, their prosthetic Fujitsu fins juggling the weight of the concept of safety. This city is light as a Frisbee is an earth -oath in a promotional pamphlet is an open mouth on sky hooks to keep the Pacific's reeling intestines down. Lest all the coast's wrath be released. The city is lumbered into place and the black bleed stoppered, overthroat. A leak that can be seen from space, spiralling, hard bloom. The replacement city never slips. Skyhooks and crab legs will keep it in place. From the proof of other kinds of veins, turn away. Tide in. Tide out. The first city was only a fiction. The second is a blurry underwater nighttime photograph, a bedtime belief you can trust. Tide in. Such a clear coast sky today: blue white like snowblindness. A perfect city slides out of you, oiled, in Pacific Standard Time.

THE AQUARIUM COLLECTOR

He starts small, assembles his aquariums before sunrise. Some would call him a hoarder, stockpiling to the hip of the sky, cubes molten in sunrise. Again and again, a creek poking a glass bone down his false arm, he reaches, shakes the nuisance, swipes a grazing ground parking lot to Clark Street, decorates land with tinfoil, viaduct, direction, *here is the steeple, here are the people.* The aquarium collector thumbs the rubberneckers that bend against the city's plexiglass cliffs, carves a cleft in the Pacific Rim for his trotting fingers, twinned pale joggers. People side by side in lanterns that gleam with salt-scraped want, as he scatters food for the drifters who rappel down the sides of reefed neighbourhoods, trade griefcalls with seagulls. Packrat, he always needs more. The aquarium collector sources his tanks from other oceans, demolished zoos, and abandoned schools, holds panes between his palms and feels the quiet promise of newness, the hum of construction. It's easy to start over, lay down a new ocean floor, rippled blue and green, build upward with arms and mirrors. He strings Christmas lights, spreads his net, pushes his roller, and paints the outer walls. The aquarium collector fills his glass rooms with lives. The landlord is becoming concerned about the mess.

MORPH

Ecodensification in the memory tunnels. The elementary school once a forest that is now an amphitheatre ringed with chain-link fence and artificial grass will soon be redeveloped for condos. A worker from the city circulates quietly, stacking small flat stones in front of each FOR SALE sign on the block. A time-lapse photograph shows the block you grew up on morphed into Vancouver Specials, creatures shedding their skins and emerging, chests exploded into golems, holding their distended stomachs, faces pebbled with sweat and stucco. Look up. Where once were bridges are now aqueducts shuttling commuters to the outlying spheres in the valley, on the mountains, drifting out there along the skyline's inflatable spine. Below the stars, constellations of ski hills quilt the sky. The night is occupied by gods on invisible wires who sail above the city, surveying the territory. In one year everything changed. Streets torn out and the private insides of houses on the brown lawns: quartz chunks of fireplaces, carved doors, floorboards. At the end of the street where you live now, a family waits three days for a demolition crew, then takes the task upon itself, the father and children tearing the bricks out with their hands. Every night the streetlights flicker on and gaze down into pits papered with blueprints. A realtor appears at your door holding a bottle of beefy Zinfandel, wearing a priest's collar: *thinking about a change?*

PACIFIC BROADCAST

City of sleepwalkers, white wires hanging from our ears, but today millions of headphones play the Pacific on permanent loop. Microphones sunk deep in the harbour. Shallows filling with static. The white wires hang from our ears, spin in the light, the broadcast begins at noon. The program backed by a corporate sponsorship, but everyone forgets after the first day of programming. A circle of people break down in the intersection of Georgia and Granville on the eighth day, press their ears to the asphalt. A coffin stands upright in the centre of the intersection but nobody is paying attention. Mesmerized by the wash. Tidal pools shimmer with signals. At low tide we are sloths, don't look me in the eye. The cloud releases the ocean one microchip at a time and swallows it again. The inhabitants of this Vancouver are stored in the sky. Banking passwords, email archives, memories, bones of fish licked clean by lightning. Nobody can figure out how to turn the sound off. The Pacific broadcast is eardrum. Screens the height of buildings along Robson Street transmit hallucinations of flow. No one can finish a sentence uninterrupted. When it rains, we weep and run for cover from the torrent on the surface of our thoughts. Crowds short-circuit, embrace telephone poles in ecstasy. It's the long moan at tide change we can't bear, minds at high slack. A month and a group forms and wades into the water at Jericho: millions listen to a livestream of their breaths, old heaving, go, the chest of the horizon slumps, quiet after the deaths. The corporate sponsor pulls out. White wires heave in the eddies. Antennae search for salt. Today the ocean glows with fury, clouds speed under its skin, telegraphing nothing.

TWO

A developer built two buildings
side by side near Hornby and
Helmcken Streets: one to house the
dead, one the living. A crew nailed
clapboard over the front of the
house of the dead, sold apartments
for $1.7 million apiece in the house
of the living. Problems arose when
the living and the dead began to
wave at each other from the side
windows, throw messages carried
on the breeze, and communicate
through the pipes that provided
the two houses with water from
the reservoir in the mountains. The
house of the dead hosted all-night
parties, had a guy who could get you
anything you wanted and the oldest
functioning pop machine downtown,
a buck a can. The house of the living
had a rooftop whirlpool jacuzzi.
The house of the dead adrift in an
ocean of rumours after two guys
were found on the roof, chained to
a pipe. The story goes they couldn't
cover the rent. But many crashed
with friends in the house of the
dead. The landlord, a guy obsessed

with collecting aquariums, turned a
blind eye. In both buildings, people
crawled into their beds in exactly
the same way. No guest policy in the
house of the dead. People circulated
in the hallways for months, eating
cheese sandwiches on the fire escapes
to feel the sun drinking from the
cold priceless rain. The developer
hired a consultant to build a bridge
between the buildings and charged a
fee for inhabitants of the house of the
living to visit the house of the dead.
The house of the living was made of
steel and glass, and its inhabitants
had forgotten how to see in the dark.
The living were blunderers. The twin
buildings spun in the faint glow of
a spectral sunset. This Vancouver
opened its prospector's ocean-sized
eye. The living went back across the
bridge when they'd had enough of
suffering. Nothing to see here. The
house of the dead was condemned,
scheduled for redevelopment in 2021.
The public was welcomed to attend
a community consultation session,
but the dead were not invited. The
development notice was posted and
the dead decorated it with the names
of their friends. An artist with a grant

hung a hammock between the two
buildings. He lived in the hammock
for a month and livestreamed
from it. His piece reflected on the
Vancouver housing crisis. One
night, a windstorm blew him down
and he moved into the house of
the dead. For two weeks afterward,
Vancouver projected the footage
from his livestream onto the facades
of the houses of the living. People
watching the display forgot the house
of the dead had been condemned,
forgot about the community
consultation session, and so the
building continued as it had been.
They took better care of their home
this time, came and went mostly
at night, didn't bug the lawyers
walking up Hornby Street between
the subterranean parkades and the
courts. Everybody knew the house
of the dead was there, but it was
no longer a controversy. The dead's
living twins in the neighbouring
building never thought about them
anymore. In this Vancouver, people
could get used to anything. The
living and the dead didn't make eye
contact and used separate entrances,
because otherwise time might get

confused, buildings might shuffle a little bit to the left or right and switch positions. The apartments in the house of the living were put up for sale and changed hands regularly, but in the house of the dead were renters and squatters and the occasional translucent teenaged prophet. That was the way of the city, spreading in all directions.

THE AQUARIUM COLLECTOR #2

The aquarium collector is on a charm offensive. Every morning he roams the alleyways and beaches, searching for more room. This Vancouver is shrinking, glass homes crammed into its armpits and inlets. The aquarium collector sets his new finds along the shoreline, along the spine of the Skytrain crawling further inland every year, on the mountain ridges and the river's corrugated edge. The aquarium collector is an expert practitioner of impression management. He fills his aquariums with native shrubs, driftwood furniture, chandeliers made from seaglass sea glass and bus tickets, the old ones, the narrow yellow-and-orange strips from our childhoods, printed with the alphabet of zones. Glass forests line Marine Drive, shelter the old budget car dealerships, the curling rink, drive-thrus, the fenced-in lot with that one pink storage locker at its centre like a hand jutting out of cracked asphalt shoals. The aquarium collector, nostalgia peddler, launches some houseboats out into the middle of False Creek. Seventies palette and high school students hired to float around like stripped logs glinting in the waves. At night the aquarium collector paces the shores, prospecting alleyways, chalking tires in the rain. He'll ride this king tide into the next century.

DEVELOPMENT APPLICATION #3: FOREST OF ELECTRIC TREES

Regarding population density and homelessness and all this
     green space. The city puts out a call for proposals. The
     winning proposal is announced on a day when spring
     rain drains from pine needles in fluorescent spirals.
     The announcement is made at the head of a trail named
     Huckleberry in Pacific Spirit Park, traffic slowing to scope
     out the small gathering. The successful proposal is as follows:
     to replace the existing forest with a forest of identical height
     and reduced density, consisting of electric trees. This will
     have the added benefit of providing illumination to the area,
     with internal zones allocated to housing and municipal
     development, a mixture of rental and retail. The transition
     will begin as soon as possible, following the consultation
     period. The larger forest downtown is unrelated to this plan.
     There will be a zip line, and a research station for graduate
     students adjoining the international grove. Aerial walkways
     for educational purposes.

There are protests. A tent city is erected. The RCMP sweeps
     through at night, tugs students out of the dirt like tulip
     bulbs, and on YouTube the footage is screams and pounding
     and the fuzzy pulmonary darkness of cedars and flattened
     backpacks. More protesters arrive and build a network of
     tree houses. There's a livestream of them tasered from the
     air like ducks in flight, bodies flapping against the branches.
     The mayor decries the violence. He is into bike lanes and
     juice and the word "unceded." This brilliantly lit forest is an

occupation. The trees are wired for sound. It ends when a protester slips through the branches and breaks his neck. Then, a vigil in the rainforest, a phalanx of cops in the cedars. Placards that read THIS CLIMATE ZONE IS REAL ESTATE. A fence goes up and there are dogs. This is for the public good. Neighbours on local TV: *We need to take back our forest from the protesters.*

The trees come down, hauled away in the night, chains
    anchored to the backs of trucks. This is how quickly a forest can be disappeared. Efficiency of engines sectioning darkness, the empty circle in the core widening, the outer fringe falling to a cleared middle. Long cylindrical corpses float down the hill, roads slick as rivers carrying the past away. Cut into a cedar and it is red as human meat. The air stinks of sap, sharp tang of it, pitch on the skin that never comes off, no matter how you scrub.

The electric trees, designed by a local artist, will perform the
    same attributes of the trees that once lived here, will be embedded with lights that change with the seasons to preserve the forest's natural cycle. A new forest more sustainable than the first, as it requires no water. The animals will come back. Vancouver erects signs printed with the *hənq̓əmínəm̓* word for "tree."

Through the electric forest, secure and walkable in darkness,
    wind blows without incident or risk of falling limbs out over the inlet, the pure velocity of a single ahistorical breath.

LAND REGISTRY

Every new arrival gets
a free upload. The land app
is your personal guide
to here. Streets encrypted creases
in palms and depth
charts, satellite-mapped. Your
first road lies between index
and thumb, uploads directly
from the particle of dirt
you place on the touchscreen.
Which memory would you
like to resume? Your open
hand, intertidal zones between
forefinger and middle
peninsula. The land app
comes with three settings:
geologic time, Provincial Park,
and the begin
to forget. While the land app
scans your sample, the
tectonic anthem drifts
in your earbuds. Use with caution
or the city will peel
at its edges.
You grew up here? Nobody
stays. Swipe right
for catacomb. Place the earth
on the centre of the screen,

do not touch while the scan
is completed, do not touch
while scan is in
process, you can be an urban
explorer on your lunchbreak!
The land app colourmatches
your sample to the tastes
and lifestyle preferences
of those in your region.
Windshield you wept through
as a child, seeing scarscape
on a mountain's exposed collarbone.
I know this place
like the back of my hand.
Never much went. Any place
else. Diction is mineral.
Press your finger to the screen,
take it, take everything
you want, fingerwhorl stamped
in concrete.
When blood alley.
Your results are in:
Negative.
You were never here,
uninvited visitor
who never left.

DEVELOPMENT APPLICATION #5

70% SOLD OUT FOR 2020–SPRING MOVE-IN!

A display suite on every corner. Drop in, take off your shoes, and relax awhile. An agent will serve you a steak on a paper plate. This bed is built from glass bricks, lit from within, you sleep the blessed sleep of pixels and fireflies. You can stop in on thirteen or fourteen display suites on your walk home. A palm reader gives you a pamphlet, sits cross-legged in the cupboard under the bathroom sink, pops out with a smile. *Thank you for visiting!* The display suite next door to your home is your favourite. Your neighbours stop in every morning for coffee. It feels so normal now to stand around the limestone cherub statue drinking coffee with your neighbours, talking about how much things change but always stay the same, how the vacant glass boxes have added a theatrical magic to the block. The lights in the display suite are always burning, like the 7-11, McDonalds, night buses. The perfect cubes glow like safety lanterns, mopped of spectral fingerprints. An article in the *Vancouver Sun* interviews a developer building the first vertical village, condos in a cliff face on the north shore, and includes an ad for its open house. On impulse you take the bus over the bridge on Sunday morning, transfer to a yellow shuttle along the road overlooking the ocean. Steps hacked into the rock. The floor of the display suite is water, the wall skyline. A woman leans spread-eagled against the glass, laughs, mocking a jumper. The room is full of metal tables that drift away when touched. The realtor reaches for the cliff and meets glass instead. A child mimics her. Lying face down on the floor, you see through the uninhabited suite below to the silver breast of the Pacific.

These floating boxes fill with people like you and you could be a part of it, part of weather, dizzy with elevation. The realtor lies down next to you, arms stretched wide. "Beautiful, isn't it?" she whispers.

3.
PACIFIC STANDARD TIME

DEVELOPMENT APPLICATION #6

Memories of inhabitants are erased each morning.

I, the aquarium collector, propose a Vancouver composed entirely of museums.

Thereby resolving all issues regarding demolition of heritage houses, mute transformation of

previously rivering streets, homes, etc., rapid as hand puppets cast on a screen of paper stretched

over mountain brackets.

The interior of each room unchanging from this point forward.

Applications from any interested party to curate.

A place for historians to gather.

Kingdom of bachelor units

for the memory hosts.

THE BRIDGES

There are entire neighbourhoods you need to forgive. Streets,
    guttered
daylighted creeks, morning, and your legs still walking
home. The ocean slumps at the end of the phone line. You sold
    this friendship
to the pawnshop three different times before it finally stayed
    there.
You had the good sense to buy it back. On this city hill,
    homeowners leave computers
in the alleys for students who rove in hungry from the forests,
    who rise
with the heat from basement suites. Are you sure about leaving
    again, this time?
You can cut your ties with stories but not with certain bus stops.
    Teen-steamed glass booth
in the long wait of spinal tap rain. A waist dawning in a white
    brick
stairwell, salt under your fingernails, the morning's widow's walk
    around the seawall, gulls
chanting your name, the climb to the turret where you grew up.
The reefs of bus cables against cloudline. Bridges fencing
with tide knit the shores you step between. Friends fall through,
    chase
geographical cures, send you emails from other decades:
    remember the rainforest
endowed to transplant research? remember the elementary
    school that sank

into the water table nothing left but the monkey bars, scrap metal
   pushing out of the earth
like bones in an elephant graveyard? remember the one among us
   who drowned between
the bridges it was dusk there was no sound that night, the
   temperate month-long fogs
climate-controlled to the drag of your blood, remember his voice
   swirling under the rockshelf boundary of knowing?
Your first teenaged lover waits for weeks before writing back:
If you think you hate Vancouver, you probably just hate yourself.

HOW TO GROW UP IN AN EARTHQUAKE ZONE

Drop duck cover. Hold your
childhood between your
knees bound by arms.

> Earthquake of a room of eight-year-old fists on
> linoleum. Foundation revolt. Tremors stroke
> the whites
> of your wrists. Go home to your ankles.
> Wait for the rocking
> to stop.

Wait,
water table.
You know this.

> Palms flat lineless open between shoulder and
> neck and mountain. The teacher who leads the
> drill bows in prayer.
> All of you, crawling toward geography.
> The ocean licks the feet
> of the cracked school steps.
> You sneak looks at the others.
> One kid's crying, his crotch soaked, forehead to
> floor.
> *Sissy.*

Instructions:
you could be thrown

from your seat
without warning
at any moment.

This is just a drill.

Playground gossip
trades in apocalypse.
Tsunami in third period.

> *This whole place won't even crumble,*
> *it'll just sink.*
> *Did you know. Ten feet down it's all water.*
> *Wasn't even enough clay for a*
> *foundation, they had to truck in the gravel*
> *from Chilliwack.*
> *And it leaks. That why*
> *there's no class in the summer.*
> *That's when they drain the whole thing off.*
> The conspiracy theorist, the pure white
> credibility of new Nike Airs.

Bind your fingers behind your neck
like it matters.
Decoy sirens sing from the roof,
paid by the insurance agency and by
the school gods, voices vaulting
over the volleyball court, chain-link reefs,
tide out on the soccer fields,
muck chalk bog.
One big shake and
              it'll all come in.

High chrome voice blasting to open sea, coast
crier, place your earlobe against the ball
of your knee and hear waves. Protect your head,
curl in, become shell.

This is the best emergency
preparedness training
you will ever get.

The classmate who pissed himself
puts up his hand.
*Why do we have to get under the desks if the
earthquake's going to be so big?*

To have something to hold on to.

Water finds its own level anyway.

Faultlines will cleave
and the ocean will rise
like a reinflated lung.

You will be ready.

THE POSTCARD ARTIST

Walking alone one night in Gastown, I am confronted by a man selling his paintings on the sidewalk. They are, when I look closely, embellishments of standard Vancouver postcards. He's drawn faces, wings, sprawling tendrils, over the clichéd images of my hometown dealt to tourists like Joker cards, and he's selling them for twenty bucks each. "Are you kidding me?" I say, and he shrugs, laughs, indicates with a sweep of his hand how many he's sold today. I pick one up and scrutinize it. City Hall, the huge statue of an explorer or mayor out front. The man has carefully glued an outsized raven's head where the man's head used to be, a grotesque transformer poised, and the edges of the card rubbed in with hot pink highlighter, like a martian forest fire, a supernova, or the irradiated presence of a ghost. In another, a woman's form is sketched in English Bay, the oil tankers crowded in her uterus, her eyes shine with black diamond luck. In another, salmon clamber up and down the cherry blossom trees, and in twilight their bones are whittled silver. On impulse, I buy them all, his whole stock.

> "What do I get from you?" he says. "What good are you
> for this city?"

The next night, I give him some of my stories.

> "A writer," he laughs. "Fiddling while Rome burns."

SIGHTING ON DAVIE STREET

"If only the rain were gasoline, your tongue
a lit match, & you can change without disappearing"
                —*Ocean Vuong, "Anaphora as Coping Mechanism"*

If only

        you'd changed into a story

before the last time I saw you

        at Seymour & Davie

If only

the rain were gasoline.

        Tumblers through the opening into the third
        accidental decade of life.

I saw you at a friend's party 2 weeks after your death

        between bodies.
        I took a photo of gulls on the beach, sundizzy with

news to teach myself about ephemeral   *your tongue a lit match*

        Wings wave
        at the back of the ocean's mouth.

An attempt, and
words give off edges like cough on pavement.

I have known too many people
my own age who have died in this
Vancouver,

hot in the patchwork under the street lamps.
Mostly reasons are not retrieved from the Pacific.
Your wake ended mid-afternoon,

solar flares in the gutter,

paper streamers dragging from my arms,

an old friend's apartment on every corner.

I could not recognize Main & Broadway.
Red storage container on the roof,
congee place open till 4 a.m.,
pancake place that burned down.
Home is a teenaged thrift store
& you can change without disappearing.

What a relief you died by truth serum.

The city is full of beaches pockets to slip bodies into,

attempts at spaces for thinking,

more of this more of this more of this loss moving into

all my narrow places.

SEASONAL AFFECTIVE DISORDER

This is the winter you teach yourself to make perfect truffles
and finish 10,000-piece puzzles. It's always midnight in your
blood. Come over, I will sit in the lap of a blue-light lamp and
show you my tropical plant poses. Downward dendrite. In my
bedroom below sea level, ceiling pillowing with moon leak.
The internet traded my personality for a bear's, I will get to
the paperwork later to have myself returned to me, in May
I will surface from the basket strainer in your kitchen sink
holding daisies and an apology note, where did we go, weather
changelings, disappearance artists. You threw a house party in
a rain barrel with a bottle of kraken rum and your mute twin
named November. Pale traitors, we face each other in a coffee
shop. Begrudge air. Seasons wrapped in sheets. I hate ducks
being joyful in the rain the way I hate extroverts at professional
development workshops. I know, I know. The rain's murmur
is the other half of every conversation. Old friend slides a
drainpipe down your shirt. Let the water go. Stay busy. Green
shoots rise in your eyes. The soil black with your mouth. Born
and raised on salt. I'm sorry I went away. Then the sun cracks
one day, any day, cracks, you empty out and float above me, call
down, "I'm in love!" The sky confesses its light. Water firehoses
from each of your toes. Lichen on your cheeks.

BASEMENT SUITE
OF PRAIRIE EXPAT

By February, the sun longs for a water birth. You tell me you're moving back to Calgary because you can't take the darkness anymore. You've been in Vancouver three years, in a basement suite on the east side. *The weather here does that to everybody. If you didn't grow up here you never really adjust.* You tell me you had no idea what you were signing up for, like a person moving to a magical realm. Cold as fuck back there. You tried every cure—vitamin D pills, a hundred-dollar blue-light lamp from Costco—and every morning stood at the windows absorbing sunlight, flower exile. You shadowed days with the diligence of a homeopath vampire. I reassure you: *The ocean holds its own bright worrystone light. Spring arrives in one day, leaps from behind a door, waving its arms. Waiting for the first signs of change will only make you feel worse.* You talk about the weather as though it's a toxic ex-lover, a gaslighter who never lets go. The bait and switch. You thought it would be beautiful. You will take nothing with soft edges back with you to Alberta.

the city used to be a rainforest

if you can't learn to breathe like a tree

you'll never make it

FROM

This street
written into you.
Decades
seen through
salt-scarred bus windows
yellow stripes on the floor
of the ocean. Gear shift
a waterfall.
Twin grooves
in pavement.
What happened here?
Where logs were
dragged to the harbour,
where bodies were dragged.

Leave and return
for your blue shoulders
glowing in the sky,
right where you left them.
That man has been standing
on that corner
for two hundred years,
looking for ships,
in that jacket.
Since the coast
made eye contact
with industries of fire
and flesh.

A tiny parade of first-graders
marches down the centre
of Granville Street
in scuba gear, handing out
hundred-dollar bills. Ever since
the city rerouted the bus and
put in palm trees,
bamboo patios, a faux forest
eyesore. Absurdity is in the espresso;
poverty in the varnish.

A taxi bargains with seagulls,
is carried away
by the screaming flock,
yellow carcass picked clean
on a rooftop for hubcaps
and details.

From above,
the mountains are
so clear, their bases
stretching under the inlet
the deep roots of teeth.

Photosensitive milklines under
sheltering reefs of microchips.
Tricky shoals of permanent
construction zone, below
smokework climate renovation and
the next century
of elephant
fentanyl.

PICKTON

you are in grade twelve

                when the news breaks

a man's face pencilled inside

                a camera grainy serial

killer working women like news

                does every writer who grew up
                here

remember the day their vancouver

                became a horror story?

ARCHIPELAGO COMMUTER IN FLU SEASON

Two people blacked out beside me on public transit three days apart a man and a woman both in their twenties bodies slight standing eyes closed then open against the grey-speckled plastic floor *what stop am I at* train shuffling with seagull backpacks packing us in make way for the fallen

Get home in the dark leave before dawn a body under the quilt moors me weighs the morning my lover falls down on public transit into my arms we fall together and she pins me against the floor faints in afternoon coffee breaks I leave in the dark again first light and a body a day collapses soundless in the crowd the transit cop steps through the steel trap opening and yells *somebody on this train pressed the silent alarm*

A day fell on me into my open arms on my chest I held it like a welcome body it slid away no warning I turned and watched it pitch its soft head under our quilt the train slipped under the lid of the earth fluorescent lit worm we held each other in travel commuters in sleep I get home in the yawn of streetlights mouth in my pocket gnawing at my palm I get home in the dark leave before dawn and one of us was falling

I held my lover in my arms on public transit today tranquilizers airlock swaying crowds held their shape at the same moment everybody on the train agreed to close our eyes and go to sleep none of us went to work *let her sleep* the speaker system played lullabies a catfish briefcase was my pillow I stuck my feet out the yellow-taped emergency exit window and touched the tunnel

wall with my steel-reinforced toes eventually the lights went out
cellphones shimmered and sang canaries sipped on our dreams
we rested we hovered

A CYCLIST'S DREAM

I live for my bike, sleep with it, haul it over me, slopejoints, bones hollow as a bird's. Rainmonths drag a jacket over, a spiny tarped cave, the water ankles me, I lie cross-legged in the centre of a city drain. I see shadows of gulls in filigreed shoes, a season somersaults down the gutter, head over heels for archipelagos, puddles in the city's linked stomachs. Anchoring wobblecups of lamplight grease, I have this diagonal cage between my weather and cold, my blue eye spins like a weather vane, on its side my bike my lover tells time I ask it questions tick tock tock tock another finger crosses my eye, the moon unleashes one more eye. Day crawls with us, soldiers in our helmets, roads margined for our elbows, halogen handlebars sweep down riverbed slopes, at dusk the streets roam with slim-heeled cyclopses. We race turbines, peel wings off rain. Six or seven nightfall I get lonely for it, math of its pedal at my hip, a bolted wrist held respectfully high. The animal above grows into you, limbs can perform any task. It's good exercise to stay awake during sleep. Dawn fingers me light-headed, my bike filter prisming this wake, the sun hurls jackets packed with tin sparrows at my eyes. Pry it off, push we push off tuck the streets up, deft, cars vanish me. Tie a tendon around False Creek for good luck, I will never be this bruised again, and free.

INTERSECTION

Nobody stopped to watch. They
erected a coffin in the centre of the
intersection at Granville and Georgia
while the Missing Women's Inquiry
was taking place in the office towers
above. When I walked to work from
the train station, the coffin was
surrounded by a zoo of commuters,
suits, some protesters. Three
concentric rings around the coffin:
placards, navy police uniforms, then
the scarves and blankly beaming
screens of passersby who had come
to warm their hands in the glow of
tragedy, or were only curious. Maybe
they didn't know what they were
looking at. Cold-weather tourists.
The news was everywhere.

I lingered every morning for as long
as I could before making myself late,
saw the lid of the coffin sway gently,
almost imperceptibly, like a porch
screen door in soft wind. I squinted,
realized I was seeing things. I stared
at it hard, but in the way these
things usually work, the lid didn't
move again. Most people rushed by

without glancing at the coffin in the
centre of the intersection. The coffin
had been there for a few days now.
High above, behind the mirrored
windows, the Inquiry about the
missing women was in session. The
panels drifted, clouds both passive
and writhing. The people in business
suits, eyes magnetized to their phone
screens, passed the upright coffin.
Students from an art college took
photos in a group. *This is someone's
class assignment.* What more could
be made? Posters of faces of missing
women pasted to the pavement
by rainfall. I stepped on a face
accidentally and jerked my foot away,
touched, burned.

There could be no coffin on its end
in the intersection at Granville and
Georgia, or any other object placed
there. A lamppost, an artificial palm
tree, a tree of unseasonal orange
or gold. A signpost to an other,
imaginary world. A kingdom where
a murderer is followed in a tidy
circle for years by officials holding
umbrellas.

The coffin towered over the people—
it was the coffin of a surreally tall
person. Was this even the coffin of
a woman? This coffin belonged to
the many women who had been
disappeared in the neighbourhood
down the sloping street, past the
street of stone with small glass tiles.

One day during my lunchbreak I
walked over to visit the coffin. A row
of food carts fed the mixed lineups of
police officers and elders with drums.
Sage blew up with the leaves and
faint salt from the distant ocean, the
way some days the whole city smells
like salt, as if when the wind blows
right you were born here on this
street corner. The coffin was made
of cardboard, I thought, but when I
drifted closer, saw it was lightweight
wood. Someone was drumming.
Traffic steered itself away from public
shame. Sometimes when I visited, I
saw people I knew, and we waved to
each other, but never moved closer
than that.

A coffin was erected at the
intersection of Granville and George.
It had no size, no depth, an open

space without insides or walls. The
coffin stood with its door open,
beckoning, *come in, come in.*

Women walked into it and did
not come back out. A coffin at
the intersection of Granville and
Georgia. By my evening commute, its
shadow had rotated. The next week,
it was gone. The inquiry was over.

EMILY

me & J went to the exhibit of
contemporary artists' responses to
Emily Carr last week at the big old
gallery downtown—artists answering
Emily with photo installations,
bluescreens, koans tacked to white
box walls—walked into the main
room and the noise was deafening—
one hundred competing voices
scrubbing each other's teeth—with
dealings and wishes—a networking
event for young lawyers hosted by
the gallery—narrow flute glasses
against the blank canvases of formal
shirts—light through white wine—a
man in his early thirties hissed *value
lives in upstream interventions*—
and behind him the electric blue
sea yawned through an opening in
treetops—the photographer must
have lain in the moss on the forest
floor to get the shot—lucite sky and
impenetrable close-up of a cone—
matrix industrial hulk—aggressive
networking cerulean digital sway
all around—Emily goddess of
representation in any childhood
allocated to the public education

system on this coast—her trees sway
in a forest preserved in a memory
biodome rooted in the highest
point of the city—in photos she is
sturdy unsmiling upholstered by
ancient coats a caravan and maybe
an exotic pet though memories do
lie and paintings too—aestheticism
kills itself before the facts of the
rainforest's massacre—suits and
polished shoes a forest impossible
to weave through—must push
into the bodies to escape—no art
visible just the black grove of formal
wear—Emily did not care so much
about humans—in elementary
school the forced trips to her floor
of the gallery—her unleashed living
trees—growling and exorcism in the
bush—brush strokes on the skull's
interior—childhood old-growth
oils—the province being sheared of
these giants then but we were not
taken there to look at paintings of
clear-cuts and mountain erosion—
trucks scooping up valleys in the
night—what possessed her green—to
know our place we should have been
shown the scarscape the erosion
and black rivers—but no only Emily
always Emily on the top floor of the

gallery her trees raising their arms
like ghosts—her face blunt giving
nothing away—cedar—me and J
broke away into the next room—
so quiet—so white—laughing at
people in the trees—the voices of
the lawyers running off the walls—
in the next room—one of her
paintings—waiting—a cedar flying
in storm—branches breaking apart
in light—writhing—releasing its
full world of dark futures—Emily if
you were here now, what would you
paint?—the ancient trees gone—
scarscape—moonscape—headwaters
blooming black carrying logs down
to the metropolis—a whale born
with no skin—J and me kept walking
and crossed a glassed-in skybridge I'd
never noticed before—must've been
a new addition—I can never keep
track of these things—renovation,
development, and demolition
are interchangeable terms in my
hometown—from the skybridge we
saw the whole city, the mountains
and ocean embracing on one of those
acid dream May nights—when the
ocean shakes—and we emerged into
a whitebox gallery so high—above
everything—and I gasped—the room

full of illuminated boxes mounted
transparent photographs of razed
mountainsides—the skin of cedars
torn back exposing red—a video of
a forest of trees exploded—making
way for expansion—

4.
INVISIBLE CITY

WALLPAPER

the panels float side by side

                  resize to the proportions of the mountains

hang against a backdrop of digital prowl

                  desktop cerulean oil eye

the frames flow hour by hour

                  by hour the wind pushes the pattern into

a generation of wind the gulf stream

                  up from a bright dream ocean homepage

the dream makes space for building

                  the city is the planet as seen from space

the towers hang apart from clouds

                  pixels in the shoals of weak signal

sky set to rotate

                  in the recording eye

panels glide overhead

                  hung on trapeze wires the city floats

among the tides

                        album automatic

cities rearrange themselves

                        permanent drift

CLOCK

In the centre of the city, a house built of fishbones and compasses. People visit to hear news from the future. Water pours into a basin in the centre of the floor through a gap in the roof. Every few years, the caretaker turns the heat up a few degrees. Visitors buy compasses made of salt and drop them into the ocean. Vancouver is sinking.

NOVEMBER TOURNIQUET

In deep fall we turn into ghosts or extend olive branches. Seasons clot us, cluster us, husky with hair. Last summer's forest fire bounces emails off our cloud armour, our shrug tectonic. Streets shape-shift under rain's snakework. Buildings rub their clay-slipped chests together until winter. Until wet lifts, vanishes us. We surrender our genie coefficients to calendar art. Someone is painting murals on the waterfalls again, someone is building a parking lot on a graveyard, someone is weaving cedar into chain-link and planting a tree on a building to mean skyline. Our shoulders have risen to water level in storms we assembled from junkyard pedigree. Nightly a foghorn sounds from the bottom of an alley stairwell's left earlobe, freighter pendant belly-up, a sleeper hit mouthing oiled words. The police are raiding shopping carts again, eight jackets reach open-armed across the intersection, crows stride the fingerbridges swing claws in eye-yellow rings around the climate loophole we crouch in. Around the peak of the house, rain frames another peak. Half-shut, our eyes guide us through the ocean-or-sky palindrome, the slick watch strap binding mountain to knee. Weather is our tourniquet.

THE FISHERMEN

Into the back passages fishermen cast their lines. Inlet economy,
this street boom or bust, lines drag the sparkling
backs of downpipes, lift soft-bodied fixes. Sometimes a belly slit
open on rogue brick and it snows down. The lines are tested.
The fishermen stand at the windows, preparing their hooks. Faces buoy
below in borders of soaked yellow rope, dim lanes. Wrought arms over
the razored stones, the fishermen strain for the shallows, cast their lines
into the lip of another bag of phosphorescent meat, haul it from the
    ocean's
eclipse at the foot of the tracks, dawn through the floorboards
like riptide. The poles whip and whistle, tradewinds splash windowsills
barnacled with waiting. Do you see it, let the line go slack and play it
safe, was that a tug. Three tugs for haul it in, one for drop the money,
they reel up and hold the thudding quota to their chests.
Pacific wades into bloodstreams, dissolves many-fisted.
At first light the cobblestones glazed with cellular residue. The
    fishermen surf
their catch over the black walls sideways with rain. A gull screams
the signal and a fish vanishes into a window's open hand, the bird
passes,
wingtip to alley membrane. A hang-glider hushes past on electrical
    wires.
The fish rise. The fishermen stand and poles watch the park.
The fishermen fill their nets. Once in a while a woman's body comes up.
They throw it back. Kiss their windows to the traffic tide,
remove their boots for the day.

GATEWAY TO THE PACIFIC

A shadow walks in. A bird walks out. A tanker walks in. A fish farm walks out. A sister walks in. A brother walks out. A kelp bed walks in. A house walks out. A stone walks in. A grave walks out. An industry walks in. A mist walks out. A friend walks in. Answers walks out. A postcard walks in. A city walks out. A lover walks in. A ghost walks out. A river walks in. A street walks out. A seagull walks in. An echo walks out. A knowing walks in. A wind walks out. Shallows walk in. An open palm walks out. A skeleton walks in. A key walks out. A prayer walks in. A signal walks out. A fish walks in. A mutant walks out. A bus walks in. A canoe walks out. A sidewalk walks in. A vein walks out. A bypass walks in. A village walks out. A bottle walks in. A person walks out. An explosion walks in. A bank walks out. Fears walk in and a woman runs out into your open mouth. A beach walks in. A hip bone walks out. A sister walks in. A brother walks out. A breast walks in. A mountain walks out. A high-rise walks in. A tree walks out. A politician walks in. A raven walks out. A raving walks in. A dream walks out. A wall walks in. A sunrise walks out. Words walk in.

SURVEYOR'S MAP

Ferns and rats and seagulls roam the cantilevered passageways and decide who this Vancouver belongs to. The apparition of a sun-stunned bird belies the grid and the ocean overhead blooms with a sunrise fresh as a tanker's aneurysm in late August. This Vancouver's second floor is held up with a winch. The rats have taken the rest and the water table is set for dinner. Underneath it all, a catacomb where currents of tissue do commerce with ancient whale roads. Marks are carved in the books of shores, long-tongued grooves where bodies were dragged down with the timbers for counting.

CITIES AND THE DEAD

What distinguishes this Vancouver from other Vancouvers is water instead of pavement. Streets flow silently, endless multiplying tributaries, algae circling the ankles of inhabitants. People make their way around the city in boats and on bicycles with paddles bolted to the wheels. The poor swim. When the alarm sounds, the tide rises. At night, from your balcony, you see people treading water, drifting past. There's a rumour that the police drag the canals for bodies before sunrise. The moon controls what this Vancouver conceals and reveals. Mysterious and relentless as money, the moonlight buffers, a million eyes whirl in the wake of tourist motorboats searching for the dock of the private hotel with its own orca. In summer the water streets are bathtub-warm. In winter the ocean curls its muscles and the black tide churns in the pipes, on doorsteps, on the bottom rungs of fire escapes. The young are moving away—why stay in this aquatic anomaly, shimmering land of childhood? Leave it to the rich and the tourists, the gigantic inflatable whales in the new harbour, the motorboat drivers who hang out on the docks and sing that song by Destroyer you used to love, the one about idols and forgetting and betrayal and home.

MONSOON SEASON STARTS IN OCTOBER HERE

This Vancouver dreams, floating in a halogen-lit poisoned watershed. Endowment Lands suspended on cables, black basket in the sky above the university on the peninsula. The storm blows in and the forest blows out, flies over the bay, searching for a landing pad. Stanley Park, moored to the high-rises, slips further over the cliff every year, roots losing their grip. Parks are strung on zip lines. Birds oasis-hop. Storm warning and the city's dozens of hanging gardens weep and break. Cedars fly upwards, flip inside-out, hold their dark arms high. Lightning dives backs of glass towers. Trapped birds fly around in the bowl above the city. In the Endowment Lands a jogger reaches her arms into a prehistoric fern and is never seen again. It's in the papers for weeks. The gutters surge with hypotheses about her whereabouts as the streets fill with drippings, a reservoir tapped from the mountain's belly where tycoons lay with orcas in ballrooms under the bedrock. After the storm, its carnage, the city's residents line the shores, swallowing driftwood.

PUBLIC TRANSIT

Walk stripped to the waist into the rivering people, never look back, door lasered neat in aluminum surf, flesh striving to dinner tables, sloughing intent. We travel in airborne chambers—*I wonder if there will be people farms after all the fish farms run out,* a child demands of the commuters—claw at rubber loops, sway like reeds whipped rush-hour raw. The traffic does not seal behind you, but swings, swings to diurnal clock. We may be a city of transients, *you'll never meet a person who was born and stays,* but seaweed knots in our elbow hinges, sand coagulates dampened with our sweat, we ride each other's blasted auras at high slack. More intertidal zone than holding ground. A woman panhandling at the commuter train station snarls at me, *one day you're gonna get it.* Coins bless our foreheads as we board the light rail across the river filleted by another morning, puzzle horizon of logging on islands, matchsticks mapping the water, we squint hard into the western light before the plunge into the undercarriage that rats and birds walk at night. A friend visits his city of birth-canal streets, I lean through the gateway and say, *from here on in it's all death and babies.* He goes to a dry place. *This train is for Waterfront terminus station.* On morning radio the hosts marvel: a whale swam under the Burrard Street Bridge, fooling us again.

THE SHY BUILDING

The shy building tires of being asked, *where's your shadow?* The reason is partly morning, partly tide. A waterfall in slow steel, the shy building bends in the pure September light, slides funhouse mirrors over the mountains, returns to position for nightfall. Above cloudcover, a sunspot burrows into your retina. The shy building, in fog, is an arm waving above the waves slipping. At sunset, it builds a bridge between the living and the dead. Inhabitants wander back and forth, looking for shelter. Sometimes a week can go by without anyone seeing the shy building. It wanders to the left into an extension of mist adjacent to the shore where, maybe, another city lurks in tidal flats. The people who live in the shy building are the same. Nomads, malcontents, undesirables. Sometimes the shy building can't be found and their mail washes up in the Himalayan blackberries strangling the rocks. TVs turn on one by one like rescue flares. People who've seen the shy building from the ocean thought it a mirage or part of an oil rig or an eccentric millionaire's floating glass library. In this Vancouver, every building has a twin.

THE WOODWARD'S BUILDING WILL BE REDEVELOPED WITH A SPECIFIC CUSTOMER IN MIND

The wood ward is where the women are kept. *Thuja plicata. Western red cedar.* Bureaucratic oat in fibre labyrinth. Story in red rings. The wood ward fits in the corner of your living space. You hardly notice it's there. *Picea sitchensis. Sitka spruce.* Inquiry is district, the hundred-year-old abattoir and temporary prison in Hastings Park refurbished with roller coasters. Put yourself in her shoes for a second but do not walk alone. Innersole empathy, history buoyant under your footsteps. *Salix lucida. Pacific willow.* Say the name, a list of species unmatched in city construction, milled to fit any foundation or argument. Grows naturally in its environment, swells internally when left to mature. *Quercus robur. English oak (introduced species).* Industrial scrap, a body seen by a neighbour, hook hung, hand-spun mobile. Review the dark grove of newspaper faces sealed with sap. Pearlescent, your smile belies your forested origins. *Arbutus menziesii. Common arbutus.* Brick crumbles under your fingers as does wood. Blood circulates through straight veins. A ring is sorted from dirt. *Cornus occidentalis. Western flowering dogwood.* The first rule of Boys Club is never talk about Boys Club. And do not. Hide behind the newspaper box to see again. News breaking this day. *Taxus brevifolia.* Western you.

THE FLOAT HOUSE

For my birthday, a friend gave me
a gift certificate to the float house
that opened not long ago on Water
Street, where the detoxes and shelters
fight luxury condos for space.
"Something you'd never buy for
yourself," she said, smiling proudly,
a person doing a good deed. She'd
gone several times, she told me,
each a "mystical" experience. As
soon as she said "mystical," my mind
began to generate excuses. I lost the
gift certificate, was prone to minor
seizures, was pregnant! The float
house was where she went to really
let go, she told me. In a dim room,
you climb into a tank of richly salted
water, never quite touch bottom.
You don't bob up either, but just sort
of drift. Lose track of time. You can
ask that music be piped in but she
found it really ruined the experience.
You just lose track, that's the point. I
checked out the website and read the
testimonials in peach-coloured font.
At least two people used the word
"mystical." I could *design my own
relaxation experience,* select lighting,

intensity of temperature, the option
of a deeper tank, the "force of the
float." The float tank had changed
one woman's life, gave her a "place
away from it all," like "an island
getaway inside the city." You couldn't
understand it until you tried it. After
about a week, I called the number
on the back of my gift certificate
and a clarinet answered. The
clarinet asked how she could assist
in satisfying my relaxation needs. I
blurted, "It's my first time," and the
clarinet said, "Mmmmmmmmh."
She congratulated me on starting
my journey and I felt soothed and
satisfied and confused, as if she had
praised me for chewing my food. We
made an appointment. I arrived at
the float house late on a Wednesday
afternoon. It was located near the old
harbour, where people sold blocks
of cheese and windbreakers on
blankets spread out in front of condo
developments named for rock—
Granite, Slate, Limestone—as if the
city were returning to its original
materials, but in name only. Etched
into the glass of the front window
in looping cursive: *Drift away...*
Like a surreal travellist agency to

an alternate realm. *The first one's free,* a cartoon snake might tell me, blowing smoke rings into my face. Over the last three or four years, this is the kind of space that multiplied in the area—thin-crust pizzerias, tap houses, cafés with board games stacked on brick window ledges. Endless editorials in the local papers argued there would be no housing by the time it was over but the construction persists. I pushed the door open and stepped inside. A bell sounded to mark my arrival. It was dark and I felt a light hand on my wrist. The clarinet said, "Your room is right this way, follow me," and I followed her. We walked down a long, dim, curving hall. "What kind of music would you like for your float?" she murmured, and because I suddenly couldn't remember any music, I responded, "Anything you want." She said, "Wavesongs are very popular right now," and in the dimness I felt myself nod. We were in my room now. Circular, with glass brick close to the floor and a faint blue light showing through. In the centre of the room the tank loomed. "When you've undressed,

climb the ladder and enter through
the hatch. It will close automatically
above you." I could barely see her
white face. "Is that safe?" I asked.
"Oh, it's all fully automated and
intuitive." I remembered my friend,
her enthusiasm, *it's like nothing
you've ever experienced, everything
just falls away.* I heard a door close.
I realized I was alone. I stripped to
my bathing suit, felt my way forward
and climbed. I could smell the water
before my body entered it. Smooth,
and a surprise when I sank for a
moment, was raised by the salt.
Antigravity. I smiled. The wavesong
soundtrack began. Darkness, the
hatch closed. Held by the dark heat,
I did not notice the light leaving
the chamber, was nourished by the
electric hum of an unseeable ancient
ocean around me. This is forgetting.

BEACHCOMBER'S DIARY: SPANISH BANKS

"On March 18, seven days after an earthquake and tsunami triggered eventual nuclear meltdowns at the Fukushima Daiichi plant in Japan, the first radioactive material wafted over...[to] Vancouver Island." —The Georgia Straight, 2011

Fish 1

Every day I walk this beach to track the radiation at the edge of our glowing city, pick up the detritus. Under the sweeping. The fallout comes in. Broom of the whole shaking. Brings another wave from the water full of it. I am the only recipient now. Study the sockets. Read the expression in the bone, fish's frail face, and fin and sand is flesh. Hold it. Press it. I come here every morning to clear it away. To receive and clear away. Tide in. What is it that eats the last thing. Only itself. But I am here to receive it. The shadow the ocean casts reflects the largeness of its flesh. Shadow swims from previous body. Tide out. Vast eye, hollow is largest. I find them, embedded, half-buried, always tucked into the sheets of sand, the face is sharpest. I clear them. Tide in. Neck broken, handful of branches. No sacrifice emerges from these waters of its own volition. Tin can, glass float, corroded trash, omens. I walk this beach and write the names of the dead in ledgers. Tide out.

Fish 2

Another four bodies today, into my hands, nuclear grifter. Rot down to orange spine, silver coarseness. Tide in. Clear and place them in the box with the others. Under skin, memory. The solid of the indestructible memory. I dream their arrival. Herds sink to the floor of a screaming ocean and crawl to me for rest. Red fingers in the crevices. Tide out. The ocean here this morning, but altered. Levitates over me, a dream of the future. Leaves nothing. Takes nothing. Somebody is living on this beach. I encounter no one but the odd man placing his aquariums in the surf. I walk and gather and the face on this one, salmon beak. Can you see it? What is. This fish has given up its eyes to what is doing the eating. All offerings from the same hand are the same. Bone the simple story and line. Skin rubs off to pure colour, a stain that will not leave my fingers, a red that does not run out. Vancouver drinks its atomic forecast. Pure energy holds the buildings up, castle dream. Tide in.

Bird 1

The nuclear tide slurps up feathers, gently sucks the body from its coat, and the coast wears a collar of soft things and spiky things harvested from the die-off. Tide out. Today the ocean sweats, marbled belly to black curtain, hydroplanes light. Down from bloom, imagination of ending. I walk it and clear it. Someone is living on this beach. This one and its almost living bronze. No softness without the living. Shadows stay. One clothes-hanger wing outstretched. Replacement. Why study this body? Every day more. I come to Spanish Banks and pace the edge of the future.

Tide in. Outstretched. Or did it fall from the sky while I was sleeping? Did it fall from the sky it slept in while flying across the ocean? What did it see? The whole ocean quivering in its irradiated birth sack. Another to clear and the feathers are coated each in the etched grey salt of the unswimmable water. Tide out.

Bird 2

Black oversized wings. Hair. Knitted from the plastic that carpets the floor of the ocean. Wire laces the spine. Body built of small stones. This is the animal that has survived. Lay it to rest. One wing half-torn, one wing bent to match the body's plotline. Debris is a mammal, changing and sticking, breathing and climbing out of the water to where I walk and clear away. Tide in. Tide out. The Pacific is a dark recycled dream and I dream inside it when I sleep, the surf so close it pounds my chest. Waves resuscitate me. Sleepwalk to the edge and clear away before the dawn's atomic proclamation. This one is not quite dead. I can feel its breath in the globular blue-white rock, frog-heart-fast, something like warmth in it. The strategic survival of hibernation. Tide in. Superior bone, crepuscular, from the deep. Somebody is living on this beach. This one will survive.

THE AQUARIUM COLLECTOR #3

The aquarium collector walks the edges and milklines of this geography
                    now known as Vancouver
his lantern of consciousness broadening with every step he walks the lines
                    in blueprint the grid stained under earth
he litters some starter homes in the pockets of the delta and tosses a
     couple into a campground
                    he knows how small a city can be
a line of wet backpacks, a heritage hut by the sugar refinery, a viaduct's wet armpit
                    the last two hundred years in escrow
in the background, the copper replicas of trees shimmer in the cerulean data crawl
                    the aquarium collector out for a morning walk
between the aquariums the city planners have inserted shipping containers
                    since they closed down the asylum

5.
ALIAS

city   of   glass

                                        arrival   city

terminal   city

glass   arrival

                                                    terminal glass

glass arrival   city

terminal glass

                          terminal   arrival

city

                          of

                          of

                          of

ACKNOWLEDGEMENTS

Firstly and most importantly, I acknowledge that this book was written on and that I was born on, grew up on, and continue to live and work on the unceded traditional and ancestral territories of the Musqueam, Squamish, and Tsleil-Waututh peoples, the only rightful stewards and caretakers of this place now known as Vancouver. For me, no land acknowledgement can ever be enough. I am grateful for the ocean and forests that give me peace. I hope to be a respectful uninvited visitor.

This book was assembled over a number of years and pieces appeared in the following publications, many in earlier versions. I am grateful to each editor. *Branch, Descant, EVENT* (thanks, Gillian Jerome), *The Capilano Review*'s experimental fiction issue (thanks, Kim Minkus), *filling station*'s mapping issue (thanks, Oana Avasilichioaei), *DREAMLAND* (thanks, Jeremy Stewart), *Lemon Hound*'s New Vancouver Writing folio (thanks, Sina Queyras, Dina Del Bucchia, and Daniel Zomparelli), *Coast Mountain Review* (thanks, Mike Berard), *Poetry Is Dead*'s prose poetry issue (thanks, Ben Rawluk), *Best Canadian Poetry 2014*

(Tightrope Books, ed. Sonnet L'Abbé), *The Elephants* (Jordan Scott and Broc Russell), *CV2*'s Poetics of Queer issue, *Plenitude* (thanks, Andrea Routley), and the chapbook *20 Objects for the New World* (Nomados), with thanks to Meredith and Peter Quartermain. "Marpole bus loop" was long-listed for a 2015 CBC poetry prize under the title "Vancouver Whalesong."

"Land Registry" ends with the phrase "visitors who never left," in reference to settlers such as myself. I read this phrase in the program for the dance program *Flicker*, presented by Dancers of Damelahamid in 2016 at the Cultch Theatre in East Vancouver.

The title "Land Registry" refers to the fact that the Vancouver Art Gallery on Georgia Street was formerly Vancouver's Land Registry and the words *Land Registry* can still be read in the stone on the side of the building. A new gallery is in its planning stages.

The epigraph for "Sighting on Davie Street" is from Ocean Vuong's poem "Anaphora as Coping Mechanism" from his collection *Night Sky with Exit Wounds*. This poem is for the people I have known and worked with who have been lost to the ongoing opiate overdose crisis in Vancouver.

The first line of "Development application #1," "The Pacific was born today and let me tell you how," was inspired by the first line of one of my favourite songs, "Transatlanticism" by Death Cab for Cutie. Their line is "The Atlantic was born today and I'll tell you how."

In "Beachcomber's Diary," the phrase "someone is living on this beach" is inspired by a line from David Markson's *Wittgenstein's Mistress*.

The jumping-off point for "Postcard home from English Bay" was the title of Sina Queyras's sequence "Five Postcards from Jericho" in her collection *MxT* (Coach House).

Italo Calvino's *Invisible Cities,* about his hometown of Venice, was a touchstone book for me. "Cities and the dead" is written after "Argia" in *Invisible Cities.* In summer 2018 I traveled to Venice, another city of rising waters and flows of capital, and that trip influenced the final form of this book.

The context of "Marpole bus loop" is the action taken in 2012 by the Musqueam Nation to protect *cəsnaʔəm,* their village site and burial ground on the Fraser River, from development, land that was never ceded to the colonial government. Musqueam people have lived on these lands since time immemorial.

"Coffin" describes the replica coffin placed by activists and land protectors at the intersection of Granville and Georgia in downtown Vancouver during the Missing Women's Inquiry. I acknowledge and honour the many stories that have been shared with me about these disappearances during my years of mental health and addictions work in Vancouver.

My thanks to the British Columbia Arts Council for a project grant and Access Copyright Foundation's research grant program for early support of this manuscript.

Thank you to Jay MillAr and Hazel Millar of Book*hug for giving this book a home and for supporting my work.

Thank you to Karen Solie for the generous and sharply scrupulous edit. Thank you to Stuart Ross for copy-editing.

Thanks to the writers I've known over the years in Vancouver, especially Leah, Elee, Hiromi, Rabbi Hannah, Adrienne, and Amy. Thanks to Liz and Jesse for friendship and to my siblings. Thanks to Adrian, Oliver, Lucas and Momo. Thanks as always to Lorraine, for listening.

PHOTOGRAPH: JOHNNY ALAM

ALEX LESLIE was born and lives in Vancouver. She is the author of two short story collections, *We All Need to Eat*, a finalist for the 2019 Ethel Wilson Fiction Prize, and *People Who Disappear*, which was shortlisted for the 2013 Lambda Literary Award for Debut Fiction and a 2013 ReLit Award. She is also the author of the prose poetry collection, *The things I heard about you* (2014), which was shortlisted for the 2014 Robert Kroetsch Award for innovative poetry. Alex's writing has been included in the *Journey Prize Anthology*, *The Best of Canadian Poetry in English*, and in a special issue of *Granta* spotlighting Canadian writing, co-edited by Madeleine Thien and Catherine Leroux, and has received a CBC Literary Award, a Gold National Magazine Award, and the 2015 Dayne Ogilvie Prize for LGBTQ Emerging Writers.

COLOPHON

Manufactured as the first edition of
Vancouver for Beginners in the fall of 2019
by Book*hug Press.

Edited for the press by Karen Solie
Copy edited by Stuart Ross
Type + design by Kate Hargreaves

bookhugpress.ca